# SASSY FOOD

## Ja-ne de Abreu

*How to Grow and Cook Food
with Your Own Farm
Any Size
Anywhere
Any Time of Year
with
Any Budget*

Designed by Cipriano Mauricio

SASSY FOOD
Ja-ne de Abreu

Copyright © 2020, JMFDEA Press

All rights reserved. No part of this publication may be reproduced, distributed, or transmitted in any form or by any means, including photocopying, recording, or other electronic or mechanical methods, without the prior written permission of the publisher, except in the case of brief quotations embodied in critical reviews and certain other noncommercial uses permitted by copyright law. For permission requests, write to the publisher, addressed "Attention: Permissions Coordinator," at the address below.

P.O. Box 235737
Honolulu, HI 96823
jmfdeapress.com

Ordering information:
www.jmfdeapress.com

Sassy Foods, by Ja-ne de Abreu.

Hardback - ISBN 978-1-7362954-0-3
Paperback - ISBN 978-1-7362954-1-0
Ebook - ISBN 978-1-7362954-2-7

First Edition

# SASSY FOOD
## Ja-ne de Abreu

Dedicated to all farmers. They work countless hours in the hot sun, cold rain, day and night to bring us nourishment. When we hold food that was not grown by us, may we remember them and send a whisper of thanks. When we hold food that we grew, may we remember they are our inspiration.

*The magical moment of October 3, 2020 at 22:18 when the spark of an inspiration solidified into the idea to create a tangible sassy book.*

In gratitude to Claire Fallon with Hinalaniaina for sparking a thought that led to my idea to create the Eve photos, which then prompted an impulse to write this book. Also, for the suggestion to include trees and fruit, foraging, and pest control.

# SASSY FOOD
## Ja-ne de Abreu

# Contents

| | |
|---|---|
| Irresistible Introduction | 9 |
| Blissful Basics | 15 |
| WowWaterWow | 21 |
| Saucy Sprouts & Marvelous Microgreens | 30 |
| Heavenly Hydroponics & Amazing Aquaponics | 45 |
| Carefree Containers | 53 |
| Gorgeous Ground Growing | 63 |
| Thrilling Trees & Fantabulous Fruit | 72 |
| Cheerful Cultivation | 81 |
| Tantalizing Tools | 91 |
| Peaceful Pest and Disease Control | 99 |
| Honorable Harvest | 111 |
| Playful Propagation | 116 |
| Content Cleaning | 125 |
| Compassionate Composting | 129 |
| Flowy Foraging | 138 |
| Food is Music | 148 |
| Food for Thought | 166 |

# Irresistible Introduction

At the very beginning of the COVID-19 pandemic, I felt it necessary to grow some of my own fresh food. Living on an island in the middle of the Pacific left me feeling uncertain about delays in the food supply chain. As an instant quarantine farmer, I quickly discovered growing food was a wonderful positive focus that kept my 93-year-old hanai mother and me grounded while chaos constantly swirled amid the increasing craziness.

I quickly teamed up with other friends wanting to do the same for the same reason. And they are all sassy kinds of people. Sassy Food Farms is a collective who have a love of growing food (we don't REALLY have farms, but we love grandiose ideas of nature).

After a few months of having a new lifestyle that only enhanced my everyday in this time of huge challenges, I started taking friends on virtual tours of my 'farm'. Most never grew anything before, became captivated, and started planting too.

I want to share with the entire planet how all of us can grow food in our own way. I also want to share how to turn your food into music without measurements. After you read it, please buy more copies for your friends and family. Besides including them in the fun, 20% of net proceeds will go toward helping others grow their own food. Or better yet, help others grow food. I've spent every single day for the better part of a year researching, consulting with other instant quarantine farmers and professional farmers, experimenting, and growing. Both failures and successes were vital to enhance my knowledge.

Food can be grown inside or outside. It can take two days or nine months, from a small saucer to a huge pot, a tiny space in a room or an entire field. It will fill your space and meals with freshness! You can grow and eat your own food every day with a small amount of time, space, and budget. Creating your 'farm' can be easy to do, even if it's in a studio apartment with no windows.

There are many amazing women and men who have shared how to cook, farm, and garden for generations. We learn from their vast knowledge and build on their shoulders. My humble book helps demystify the confusing process of growing food. I don't know one person who is not affected by the pandemic in some way. May this visual jungle showing you how to grow edible peace bring some semblance of calm to you and your loved ones.

And because I'm Sassy with a capital S, I sprinkled Eve mod els amid gorgeous Hawai'i. Compelled to empower all feminine forms to release their inner wild, I uplift our sisters in all ages, colors, shapes, and sizes. May we ought to honor them as we honor the importance of food.

So, delve inside to experience the magic within. If you don't grow food now, by the end of this book I'm sure you won't be able to resist and will become a Sassy Food Farmer. Please join our collective at sassyfoodfarms.com.

SASSY FOOD
Ja-ne de Abreu

# Blissfull Basics

**What?** Grow sassy food! Sassy food is natural food. No chemicals and no pesticides. It's simple and complicated at the same time. There are many ways to cultivate food. The most obvious is to have a garden or a farm. What if you live in an apartment? Yes, you can grow food and not even a balcony is needed. I will share all the different ways. Even if you live in a cave in a mountain or in a submarine at the bottom of the ocean, you can have fresh food at your fingertips. Every single person can benefit from producing something fresh. It's not just for farmers and hippies. Something special happens when you plant a seed and nurture as it grows. It is a great contrast when you harvest and eat it from eating something bought in a box. It's not bohemian to live naturally. It's natural. It was a normal way of life for our ancestors and I'm certain you'll love creating food, too.

# SASSY FOOD
Ja-ne de Abreu

Page 16

# SASSY FOOD
## Ja-ne de Abreu

**Where?** Anywhere! Outdoors is great because it uses the beautiful sun and natural elements. Indoors is also wonderful because it protects plants from pests and inclement weather. With modern technology, there are almost endless ways available. If subterranean farms can exist, you can grow something edible wherever you live or work. Imagine a break room where employees harvest their own lunch. Food can be grown on a countertop, or a table, by a windowsill, or on a balcony, in a corner in a room, in a closet, on a wall, or in a yard. It can grow in your bedroom, on your refrigerator door, on a shelf in your shower, on top of a dog crate — unleash your curiosity!

**When?** NOW! The energy you put into growing food will in turn be the energy you consume through eating it. When you care for your plants, you are eating that love. I want as many positive vibrations as I can get. Do you? So, what are you waiting for? Besides, plants use carbon dioxide to make oxygen. The more plants, the better the air quality. Let's all create our own edible jungle!

**Why?** Because you love yourself! Being in tune with nature is muffled with produce sitting around for months that is washed many times. Elevated biotics is what some claim is a coating around fresh unwashed produce. When food is grown by you, you control how you wash it. Regardless of this unsupported claim, farmers' markets are increasingly popular for a reason. The fresher the better. While only a few may be lucky enough to have a real farm, all of us can add fresh food to our meals every single day starting at a few dollars.

**How?** Read on and find out!

# WowWaterWow

Water — the source of life. We have all heard that expression before. But have we considered the depth of that statement?

Seeds would remain in their hulls. Plants wither and die without it. We as humans would also.

Produce wouldn't be clean and fresh. Same with us. How long do you last without a shower or brushing your teeth?

Overwatering has the opposite effect. Plants and humans drown from excess of this marvelous wonder.

Just like everything — balance is key.

The same water has been circulating around the globe for millions of years. It changes from steam rising to the clouds, to mist, to rain, to snow, to ice, then it melts and evaporates again. A drop of water can rest on a leaf in a lush rainforest in the Amazon and transform to become part of a huge wave in the Indian Ocean. It can float in a lazy river or fly over a roaring waterfall. The same drop of water.

It's almost magical.

Humans are made mostly of water. So are all the animals that exist here on the planet. We all can flow too.

As we begin our adventure of growing food, respecting water is important. Without it, we would not be here. Conserving clean water is essential to our existence. Some want to overlook our responsibility because it is easy to think "what can I do?"

If each of us did our part, we can affect our families and change small things around our homes. This will help communities and cities to be more sustainable. And our countries will be affected as a result. How can that do anything but change the world for the better? And in turn, we each will benefit. So yes — one person can change the world.

After all, we dance with the elements because we are made of those same elements.

**SASSY FOOD**
Ja-ne de Abreu

# Saucy Sprouts & Marvelous Microgreens

# SASSY FOOD
## Ja-ne de Abreu

The quickest and easiest food to grow is right here. It can grow in a small space, on a countertop, or a windowsill. Anywhere from two days to three weeks and you have yummy concentrated nutrition. They have higher vitamin, mineral, and antioxidant levels than their mature counterparts. Most vegetables and herbs and some grains and grasses can be eaten as sprouts or microgreens. What is the difference? Sprouts are when the seed starts to grow (germination). Microgreens are when the first leaves appear.

Just as humans, seeds are not all exactly the same. All are unique and crave to be treated specially. Some seeds grow better as sprouts and others as microgreens. Some sprouts and microgreens need a blackout time, just as they would if they were in the ground to grow into mature plants, and some don't. Simply use amber jars, cover a tray with a towel, or use the bottom of another tray as a hat. Some microgreen seeds like to be weighted during blackout time. It keeps them in the most contact with the growing medium and helps them take stronger root. Stack your trays or put any weight on top, like dumbbells. Do ten reps whenever you check on them to keep fit while watching them grow. Once they turn green, uncover, and watch them rise. Some seeds like it dry and others love it wet. Keep in mind as many seeds start sprouting, they may look like they are moldy, but it is root hair. After rinsing it, you can tell the difference. They are all delicious and freshhh! And you will be too!

When I started, I had no idea so many seeds could be grown and eaten in this way. I searched and searched and found snippets of information at a time. Here is a longer, but not complete list for you.

Adzuki bean — easy to grow, high protein. Flavor is sweet and nutty. Presoak 4-8 hours. Sprouts in 2-3 days. No blackout time. Microgreens in 7-8 days.

Alfalfa — easy to grow, good for cancer prevention and diminishing menopause symptoms. Flavor is mild and crunchy. No presoak. Sprouts in 2 days. Blackout time 3-4 days. Microgreens in 8-11 days.

Amaranth — tricky to grow. Gorgeous vibrant pink color. Flavor is earthy. No presoak. Sprouts in 2-3 days. Blackout time 4-5 days. Microgreens in 8-10 days.

Anise — easy to grow. Used for many medicinal purposes. Flavor is like licorice. No presoak. Sprouts in 2 days. Blackout time 2 days. Microgreens in 7-8 days.

Asparagus — long to grow. Presoak 4-8 hours. Sprouts in 7-8 days. No blackout time. Microgreens in 3 weeks.

Basil — best as microgreens. Many varieties with different tastes. No presoak. Sprouts in 2-3 days. Blackout time 4-5 days. Microgreens in 10-13 days.

Beet — best as microgreens. Flavor is sweeter than beets. Soak over 10 hours. Sprouts in 2-3 days. Blackout time 5-6 days Microgreens in 8-12 days. They like growing close together and to be grown under a thin layer of soil. Can grow to larger baby leaf stage.

Broccoli — easy and fast. Flavor is more mild than mature broccoli. No presoak. Sprouts in 2 days. Blackout time 4-5 days. Microgreens in 7-10 days.

Brussel Sprouts — easy and fast. Flavor is slightly bitter. No presoak. Sprouts in 2-3 days. Blackout time 3-4 days. Microgreens in 7-10 days.

Buckwheat — easy and fast. Small amount is good. Large amounts can lead to skin sensitivities. Flavor similar to lettuce. No presoak or just a few hours. Sprouts in 2-3 days. Blackout time 4-5 days. Microgreens in 7-9 days.

Cabbage — easy and fast. Flavor is mild and sweet. Presoak. Sprouts in 2-3 days. Blackout time 3-5 days. Microgreens in 8-10 days.

Carrot — slow and a little tricky. Flavor bitter. Sprouts in 2-3 days. Blackout time 4-5 days. Microgreens in 8-14 days.

Cauliflower — easy. Flavor sweet and peppery. Sprouts in 2-3 days. Blackout time 4-6 days. Microgreens in 8-12 days.

Celery — slow growing. Flavor like mature celery. Sprouts in 5-7 days. Blackout time 7-9 days. Microgreens in 13-16 days.

Chard — best as microgreens. Grow under a thin layer of soil like beets. Flavor sweet. Sprouts in 2 days. Blackout time 4-5 days. Microgreens in 8-10 days.

# SASSY FOOD
Ja-ne de Abreu

## SASSY FOOD
### Ja-ne de Abreu

Chia — Flavor bitter. Can consume just the seeds in some water or smoothie. Sprouts in 2 days. Blackout time 4-5 days. Microgreens in 10-12 days.

Chives — slow. Flavor spicy. No presoak. Sprouts in 6-9 days. Microgreens in 14-24 days.

Cilantro/Coriander/Chinese Parsley — Best as microgreens under a thin layer of soil. Flavor tangier than parsley. Recommend the quick bolt rather than slow for obvious reasons. Presoak a few hours. Sprouts in 4-6 days. Blackout time 6 days. Microgreens in 14-18 days.

Clover — easy and popular. Flavor nutty and crunchy. No presoak. Sprouts in 2 days. Blackout time 3-5 days. Microgreens in 7-12 days.

Collard — easy. Flavor similar to kale. No presoak. Sprouts in 2 days. Blackout time 4-5 days. Microgreens in 7-10 days.

Cucumber — easy and fast in cooler temperatures. No presoak. Sprouts in 2 days. Blackout time 3-4 days. Microgreens in 7-12 days.

Dandelion — easy and slow. Can grow to baby leaves. Flavor bitter. No presoak. Sprouts in 2-3 days. Blackout time 4-5 days. Microgreens in 12-25 days.

Dill — easy in cooler temperatures. Flavor tangy. Presoak. Sprouts in 4-5 days. Blackout time 4 days. Microgreens in 12-15 days.

Fava — fast to grow. Flavor similar to sunflower. Presoak overnight. Sprouts 3-4 days. Blackout time 4-5 days. Microgreens 12-15 days.

Fennel — easy to grow. Flavor like licorice. No presoak. Sprouts in 2-3 days. Blackout time 3-4 days. Microgreens in 10-14 days.

Fenugreek — quick and popular. Flavor spicy. No presoak. Sprouts in 2-3 days. Blackout time 4-5 days. Microgreens in 10-14 days.

Flax — slow. Flavor mild. No presoak. Sprouts in 2-3 days. Blackout time 4 days. Microgreens in 8-12 days.

Garbanzo — easy. Best grown as microgreens under a thin layer of soil. Flavor sweet and nutty. Presoak a few hours only or will mold. Sprouts in 2-3 days. No blackout time. Microgreens in 8-12 days. Cook these for best safety.

Garden Cress — popular. Likes less water. Flavor tangy. No presoak. Sprouts in 2 days. Blackout time 4 days. Microgreens in 8-12 days.

Kale — popular. Flavor mild, not bitter like mature plants. No presoak. Sprouts in 2-3 days. Blackout time 4 days. Microgreens in 6-10 days.

Leek — slow. Flavor intense onion. No presoak. Sprouts in 3-4 days. Blackout time 3 days. Microgreens in 10-12 days.

Lemon Balm — slow. Flavor lemon/licorice. No presoak. Sprouts in 3-4 days. Blackout time 5 days. Microgreens in 14 days or more.

Lentil — easy and popular. Flavor like peas. Presoak a few hours. Sprouts in 2-3 days. Blackout time 2 days. Microgreens in 7-12 days.

Lettuce — popular. Can grow to baby greens. Flavor mild. No presoak. Sprouts in 2-3 days. Blackout time 4 days important. Microgreens in 10-16 days.

Marjoram — easy and tiny. Flavor sweeter than oregano. No presoak. Sprouts in 2-3 days. Blackout time 3-4 days. Microgreens in 10-14 days.

Mint — tricky and fun. Flavor similar to mature plant. No presoak. Sprouts in 2-3 days. Blackout time 3 days. Microgreens in 10-14 days.

Millet — quick to mold. Flavor mild grassy. Presoak 4-8 hours. Sprouts in 2 days. Blackout time 4 days. Microgreens in 12 days or more.

Mung Bean — easy. Flavor buttery bean. Presoak 8-12 hours. Sprouts in 2 days. Blackout time 3 days. Microgreens 7-10 days.

Mustard — popular. Flavor spicy. No presoak. Sprouts in 3 days. Blackout time 3-4 days. Microgreens in 7-10 days.

Nasturtium — quick to mold. Flavor intense spicy. Presoak 4-8 hours. Sprouts in 2-3 days. Blackout time 3-4 days. Microgreens in 8-12 days.

# SASSY FOOD
Ja-ne de Abreu

Onion — slow. Rich in nutrients and needs to be used sparingly. Flavor like mature plant. no presoak. Sprouts in 3-5 days. No blackout time. Microgreens in 12-16 days. Grow hydroponically in amber jars.

Parsley — easy. Flavor milder than mature plant. Presoak. Sprouts in 5-7 days. No blackout time. Microgreens in 18-30 days.

Pea Shoots — good to stir fry. Flavor slightly nutty. Presoak. Sprouts in 2-3 days. Blackout time 3-5 days. Microgreens 8-12 days. Grows tall. Can harvest when it grows 5-10 inches.

Purslane — easy. Best as microgreens. Flavor mild spinach. No presoak. Sprouts in 3-5 days. Microgreens in 10-14 days.

Radish — easy and popular. Flavor spicy pepper. No presoak. Sprouts in 2 days. Blackout time 3-4 days. Microgreens in 8-10 days.

Rutabaga — low light. Flavor mild pepper. No presoak. Sprouts in 2-3 days Blackout time 3-4 days. Microgreens in 8-12 days.

Sage — slow. Flavor like mature plant. No presoak. Sprouts 7-10 days. No blackout time. Microgreens in 2-3 weeks.

Sesame — easy. Flavor mild. Presoak 2-4 hours. Sprouts in 2-3 days. Blackout time 3-4 days. Microgreens in 7-10 days.

Spinach — cold climate. Flavor similar to mature plant. No presoak. Sprouts in 3-5 days. Blackout time 2-3 days. Microgreens in 10-14 days.

Sunflower — popular. Best as microgreens. Flavor zesty. Presoak overnight. Sprouts in 1-2 days. Blackout time 3-4 days. Microgreens in 8-12 days. Best harvested when two leaves emerge.

Tarragon — tricky. Flavor mild licorice. No presoak. Sprouts in 3-7 days. No blackout time. Microgreens in 10-14 days.

Turnip — easy. Flavor mild and sweet. No presoak. Sprouts in 2-3 days. Blackout time 3-4 days. Microgreens in 8-12 days.

Wasabi — easy, low light. Best as microgreens. Flavor intense pepper. Presoak. Sprouts in 3-5 days. Blackout time 3-4 days. Microgreens in 2-3 weeks.

Wheatgrass — good for juicing, excellent nutrition. Flavor sweet grass. No presoak. Sprouts in 2-3 days. Microgreens in 1-2 weeks.

# SASSY FOOD
Jane de Abreu

Sprout mixes are a great way to save money and get an extra burst of complex flavor. My favorite is a bean mix containing French, green and red lentils, green peas, and mung beans. Another favorite is a spicy salad containing mustard, radish, and alfalfa. If this is something you will do forever, (which is my hope for you) buy in bulk to save money.

**Sprout supplies needed:**
Seeds (organic, non-GMO, or heirloom) + jars (usually wide mouth) + sprouting lids or a buy a complete kit.

**How to grow:**
See the list above to see if your seed needs a presoak and how long. Soak them in the jar you will use and cover it with a sprout lid. Sprout lids usually fit on wide mouth jars and have holes for air circulation and to hold seeds inside when you bathe them. When it's time, rinse them until the water runs clear. If your sprout lid has two size drain holes, take care to drain on the side best for small seeds. Place the jar upside down for a few minutes to drain all the water. Then gently shake the jar to spread the seeds around and lay it on its side. Do this process twice a day until they are ready to come out to play. Again, the length of growth time depends on the seed. Some seeds take two days and others weeks.

Some sprouters are round plastic and stack on top of one another. Some of this type automatically shower your lovelies. Place seeds, change the water once a day, and harvest. That's it! Some sprouts get a little rooty and if it's too much, cut off the ends. Use ceramic scissors to prevent edges of the stems from discoloring.

**Microgreen supplies needed:**
Seeds (organic, non-GMO, or heirloom) + trays or buy a complete kit.

**How to grow:**
Various microgreen or sprout trays come in different materials and sizes. If not using a grow light, place near a window or outside. The best trays offer a wick on the top tray and a second tray underneath to hold water. You can better monitor water levels for your lovelies. These trays can be used hydroponically, with coconut coir, or soil.

Some complete kits include a grow light so these can be grown absolutely anywhere. Seed pads are already prepared, so anyone who thinks they only kill plants can grow this! Just pop it in, add water, and you'll have food in a few days.

I love to grow sprouts and microgreens in multiple stages. For instance, one is starting, another is budding, and a third is ready to harvest. Shelves on a wall, bookshelves, or multi-tier plant stands or a wide windowsill are perfect!

*Make extra and share*

**Differences of grow medium:**
Hydroponically — add water only to trays. A grow pad or paper towel can be used for tiny seeds.

Coconut coir — a clean alternative. Rinse this well to remove any salt that can damage tender roots. It can be used for three grow cycles before recycling.

Soil — good to use organic soil mixed with perlite, coconut coir, or peat moss to fluff the soil and provide better drainage.

**Caring:**
Mist twice a day with dechlorinated water. Fresh sprouts are sensitive. Use a natural dechlorinator. A tiny bit added to a gallon of water will last a long time, unless you're growing a forest like me.

**Harvesting:**
Microgreens grown in trays — cut with ceramic scissors. It is best to cut above the soil line. They do not need a rinse, but you can if you like. Some microgreens regrow a few times and some only once.

**Eating:**
Most can be eaten raw. You get more nutrition that way. Some need a little stir fry. Heat a tiny amount of olive oil (regular), or another high heat tolerant oil, then quickly stir them in for a few seconds. Any longer, they will go limp and dark and mushy. You can still eat them, but it's not as good, both in taste and in nutrition. A little is lost with the heat. Add your own Exotica options from the instrument list in the Food is Music chapter.

# Heavenly Hydroponics & Amazing Aquaponics

**Hydroponics** uses water and nutrients in a basin to grow food. **Aquaponics** have fish in the water basin. Fish provide nutrients for plants and the plants provide nutrients for the fish.

Food grows quicker and cleaner in both systems. These can be grown in various ways in specific containers. For instance, a small pot can have an inner slatted cup that supports the plant in a water basin, or a water fountain with a smaller bowl on the top level that holds plants. There are also many larger systems that are designed for growing food.

*Many containers are made for hydropon growing.*

## Hydroponics

Indoors or outside, these systems are quite amazing. They have many clear benefits over soil growing, such as less environmental impacts, faster growing plants, and greater harvest! I turned my game night table into a support for my hydroponics garden. Since I can't have friends over during the pandemic, I care for my lovelies in the evenings instead.

Traditionally, these were tricky outdoor unattractive systems requiring almost a science degree. Now there are so many easy beautiful kits available that most can benefit from having one. They come from tiny to humungous, so pick the one that best suits your needs and budget.

Some easy to grow systems use pods. They are self contained cups with dirt, seeds, and nutrients that you pop into a water reservoir with grow lights. So simple, anyone can grow food anywhere. The ONLY thing you need to do is plug it in and add water. Watch how quickly your food grows! These units were inspired by systems that grow food in space. If food can be grown there, you can certainly grow it in your home. Future pods will be needed, so factor that into your overall costs. The variations are from three pods to several hundred in a wall system, and many in between.

Other systems use slatted cups, and others use a plastic barrier with holes that use sponges. Clay pebbles are also a popular growing medium in some systems.

It seems complicated. It's not. Check your pH levels. Optimal is between 5.5 and 6.5. Most plants still thrive on either end of the range. You can increase or decrease the pH with many nutrients and chemicals. For example, phosphoric acid will lower pH and potassium hydroxide and baking soda will increase pH.

Know what is best for your particular lovelies. If your water is soft or hard, it will affect your pH. I love growing greens. They do best between 6.0-6.5. Mint can grow up to 8.0.

Because your system is a perfect growing environment, algae will love to grow here, too. They can suck up all the nutrients and oxygen in the water, leaving your lovelies limp. Keeping any water surface covered helps keep atrocious algae away. If they try to come to the party, clean your system with food grade hydrogen peroxide. If things get out of hand, remove your plants and eat them or plant them in soil. Clean your system with a tiny amount of bleach to end the algae bloom and start over.

## Aquaponics

People think aquaponics are for people who want to eat fish and they have to be grown in huge vats outside. This is no longer true. I have a 10-gallon system on my counter with beautiful goldfish I love to watch when I'm in the kitchen. I harvest food minutes before preparing, loving to have fresh food at my fingertips. It's one of the main reasons I became an instant quarantine farmer. I feed my fish a couple of times a day, clean the tank once a week, and add an eggshell for calcium. Plants thrive with the siphoned dirty water. It's a beautiful symbiotic cycle!

I appreciate both hydroponics and aquaponics. I personally find aquaponics easier. Food grows with hardly any attention. This is because microbes convert the ammonia from the fish waste into nitrites and then into nitrates. Then plants take in the nitrates through their roots, using them as a source for plant essential nitrogen. While not having success so far growing from seed in my aquaponics system, any small plant grows wonderfully. I start seeds in a small pot system or newspaper cup. Then move them over when they are larger.

*Feed fish natural food to keep your food natural.*

# Carefree Containers

Small, large, shallow, deep, hanging, wheeled, round, square, triangle, rectangle, we all have usable containers for growing food. It doesn't have to be something specifically made for plants. You can reuse pottery, a cup, a bathtub, anything you can imagine. There are many high-tech options. Some have magnets and a grow light, so you can even stick it in your closet and grow food. Others levitate for extra zen. There are also almost uncountable different kinds of raised beds. These can be indoors or outdoors. Keyhole garden systems are a wonderful outdoor option in a corner of a yard because composting can be deposited directly inside.

Many people and companies are taking the guesswork out of growing food. Nowadays there are several kits which offer partial materials, to every single thing you need except water. Even mushroom log kits are available to grow at home. I dream of the day when growing fresh food is commonplace. I know it can easily become reality.

Materials of containers can be clay to plastic to wood to ceramic to fabric to glass to concrete. Fabric, terra cotta, and wood are best because they don't damage roots. Concrete is fun and easy to make yourself but be careful. It can heat up and retain that heat, so your plants need to love it. Plastic is a cheap option and if it's too hot, roots can get burned.

*Try a small kit to start.*

I find indoor containers having drain holes and a drain tray to be most convenient. Some containers have hydroponic grow cups with a cotton wick. Add a little soil or coconut coir and pour water in the bottom. The wick will soak up the water and water your plants as they need. It's so simple!

Outdoor containers are best with drain holes. Place a small piece of mesh and line the bottom with small rocks for better drainage.

What can be grown in these? Just about ANYTHING! It all depends on the size of the plants you want to grow.

Grow bags are great because they are inexpensive. Ones made with felt fabric provide great airflow for roots. They come in a variety of sizes. The larger sizes are a little clumsy to move around, so pick a good permanent spot. It is best to raise them off the ground so they can drain well. I use several on plant stands and in a window box with slats. Some come with a flap to harvest root vegetables. They are great for potatoes and sweet potatoes. Others attach to a wall to form a living wall. As always, be careful to check where water will drain to avoid a mess. You can buy one for under $10 or a pack of 100 for $200. With so many options in between, choose ones that are best for you.

Wooden barrel containers are a great way to reuse old wine barrels. Cut them in half and drill drain holes to grow many things! Some stores now sell them ready to plant. I put mine on wheels to make it easier to move around.

# SASSY FOOD
Ja-ne de Abreu

This year I rolled the entire container 'farm' under the carport during a hurricane threat in just a few minutes. I could never have budged my larger containers without wheels.

Grow tents are excellent to control every aspect of your environment: temperature, light, humidity. By having your 'farm' in an enclosed environment, pest control is a breeze. With all these factors at your wizard fingertips, your productivity is guaranteed to be successful! They are well known for being only used indoors, but there are outdoor systems as well. If you live in a dungeon in Antarctica, or in a barren climate, this might be the way to go to grow food year-round. They would also work well in a corner in a small apartment anywhere. They range from $50-$1,500.

Short on space? Go vertical! Some containers can house over 30 different varieties of plants. Get a lazy susan attachment or wheels to move them so all plants get sun or to have a good dance partner. Some vertical containers provide better drainage, so nutrients stay in each layer and are not washed away. They also range in price from a few dollars to several hundred, depending on size and materials.

Hanging containers are another great way to move up! A simple hook and your tomatoes or any viney plant can sway like a monkey hanging in the breeze.

There are many types of raised beds. They come in a plethora of different materials and sizes. Some are short and lay on the ground. Others are waist high. Some have wheels and others are attached with trellises. Additional positives are they provide better drainage, attract less weeds and pests, and grow food anywhere. You can grow food on a balcony, in a yard, or indoors. With so many options, prices range from $10-$2,000.

Keyhole systems are a wonderful invention designed in Africa to help sick people be able to garden. They are high enough so one doesn't have to bend down. Also, they are sturdy enough so if the sick person had to lean against it to rest a while, they could be supported. And they are small enough that one could reach all areas easily. It combines composting and raised beds. They were so productive, healthy people adopted them into their gardens. You can make your own or buy and assemble.

It is a round raised garden with a notch in the center to make it easy to access the compost. Also ingenious is the drainage system. Using up to 70% less water than in ground crops, it's perfect for drought-prone areas. Simply rotate your crops, turn over the compost, and water. Complete kits start at $200, but can you can DIY much cheaper.

# Gorgeous Ground Growing

**SASSY FOOD**
Ja-ne de Abreu

Find a nice sunny spot. Figure out what to plant and where you will grow them. Spruce up your soil. Plant. Nurture your plants. Harvest. Simple! In a perfect world. Is your world perfect? Mine's not. Let's figure out how to make your corner into an uncomplicated paradise.

If you are fortunate to have an area of Earth for your own, find a nice sunny spot, and get started. But is it too much sun? Look around and see if there's concrete or walls to provide additional heat and burn your plants. Depending on your size 'farm,' look into greenhouses or hoop houses to keep your plants fresh in the heat and/or protect it in cold snaps.

Study your ground. A nice level area that drains well is perfect. If it will flood, then pick another spot, or change your plan to raised beds.

When developing a plan, the best way to achieve success is to see what the professionals are growing. Grow local. In Hawai'i cold weather produce like cauliflower and broccoli are hard to grow. We don't have the correct climate. The ground never freezes, so bacteria in the soil doesn't die. While growing greenbeans is not a snap here, I can grow long beans instead.

Make a chart of what you will plant and where. Think of companion plants, like the three or four sisters. Consider flowers and herbs for pest control. It's easy to get excited and just stick things in the ground. But later, will you have squash overtaking your tomato plant?

# SASSY FOOD
Ja-ne de Abreu

Visualize how the plants will grow and what nutrients they will need. See if they like each other. It's important. By the way, cucumbers and tomatoes are great together as food, but miserable together as plants. We all want to be happy. So do your plants. That in turn will make you happier. Yay!

How will you water? Hose, irrigation system, olla balls, or watering can? Decide now so you won't have to backtrack later.

If you have a lawn to remove, take it out by manual removal, sheet mulching (layering), or solarization.

It's an excellent idea to know your soil. Do a soil test. If it's lacking in nutrients, condition it with amendments. Till your soil to get it fluffy. Add compost. Mulch is a great option for retaining water, keeping weeds away, and temperature control.

Plant your lovelies. Are you growing from seed? Consider making newspaper pots (they are biodegradable) to start them where you can keep careful watch. Once they are large enough, plant in the ground (or in containers).

Then watch them grow. Take a mat nearby and practice yoga. Or sit in a chair and drink a beer. Whatever works for you. They'll love the attention.

No ground to grow anything? Community gardens are a great way to share the love of growing food and meeting new friends.

SASSY FOOD

SASSY FOOD
Ja-ne de Abreu

# Thrilling Trees & Fantabulous Fruit

Trees remove carbon dioxide and are a major contributor of oxygen for our planet. It takes about eight trees to provide oxygen per person. There is a growing movement to plant more trees around the globe, so we can breathe easier and have cleaner air.

Are trees edible? The short answer yes! Some of them. Cinnamon, for instance, is the bark of a tree. The inner bark of birch, elm, fir, pine, and spruce trees are also edible. Smaller leaves from some trees like beech, birch, Chinese elm, hawthorn, linden, moringa, mulberry, and sassafras are edible. Some are tastier than others. But it's not a good idea to go around picking and eating leaves from any tree. Humans are not designed to digest cellulose from larger leaves. With so many tasty edible options of food, why would you want to anyway?

Maple syrup! That is from the sap of a maple tree boiled down over a long, long time to get to that yumminess. This also applies to birch, sycamore, and walnut trees.

Many nuts grow on trees or shrubs, like almonds, Brazil nuts, cashews, chestnuts, hazelnuts, macadamia, pecans, pine nuts (really a seed), pistachios, and walnuts.

Some of these nuts are actually drupes. Drupes have fleshy fruit with thin skin and a stone. Almonds, apricot, cherry, coconut, dates, gooseberries, longan, loquat, lychee, mangoes, nectarine, olives, peach, pecans, plums, rambutan, and walnuts fall into this category.

Blackberries and raspberries have many drupes and are called aggregate fruit. Strawberries are similar in that they are also aggregates, but they have many achenes, not drupes. And to make things more interesting, there are multiple fruits like breadfruit, figs, jackfruit, mulberry, noni, and pineapples.

To be a berry, a fruit has to have an outer skin, two or more seeds, and must develop with a flower containing one ovary. So technically, avocado, banana, blueberries, all citrus fruits, carambola (aka starfruit), coffee, cranberries, cucumbers, currants, dragon fruit (pitaya), eggplant, grapes, kiwi, melons, persimmon, pineapples, pomegranate, and tomatoes are berries.

So, does this mean an apple is a berry? They have more than two seeds and an outer skin. Nope! They, along with hawthorn, loquat, medlar, pears, and quince, are pomes. They have a 'core' difference.

# SASSY FOOD
Ja-ne de Abreu

# SASSY FOOD
Ja-ne de Abreu

Confused yet? I am! It's reminiscent of a human breaking down one's ancestry into tiny categories. That person is a beautiful human, regardless. Does it matter? To some. Why does it matter? I love beautiful humans in all their amazing sizes and colors. It doesn't matter to me where their ancestor was born. The same applies to all this beautiful food, whatever their proper categories.

Some countries use avocado for salty things like in a salad or in guacamole. Other countries eat fresh pieces with sugar over cereal or in a smoothie. Tomatoes are also used in many desserts. Why not try both ways? Maybe they each have a valid point. Learning about other cultures and their foods has helped me pleasantly surprise people with my gastronomic stories.

Some trees and fruit can grow in containers and others need to be in the ground. Climate is important.

In Hawai'i I have a macadamia nut tree in my yard. As soon as nuts fall, flowers bloom again, and a new cycle starts.

By the way, the expression tough nut must have been named after macadamia. I broke a few nut crackers trying to open these. Once I 'borrowed' my friend's old school Mac nutcracker, I could open these brutes. In New Orleans, I had a pecan tree. Pecan trees exist here, but don't produce well because they require 250 hours below 45° F. They will grow and produce some nuts, but not many. So why would I grow it here?

If you are looking for an indoor plant and have a well-lit room, consider one of these lovelies to fill a corner. Kumquat, for example, is small and grows well in a container. Look up what soil they appreciate, as well how they like water. As all plants, each is unique in their own special way. Find ones that match your climate and most important of all, you.

# Cheerful Cultivation

SASSY FOOD
Ja-ne de Abreu

The definition of cultivation is the process to acquire a skill. We are developing our plants and also ourselves in the process. We want the best for our plants, and ourselves. Like many things in life, it's good to have a plan. What to grow? It depends on where you live. Produce grown by local farmers is a good indication of what you can grow in your corner of the world. A wider variety of plants can be grown indoors because you control the climate.

Start off by acquiring good seeds. Healthy seeds make healthy plants. If purchasing plants, make sure they look good.

Plant your lovelies where they will thrive. Know if they prefer sun or shade.

Watering your plants the way they like to be watered is essential. Just dumping water on them is not desired.

Inspect your plants at least twice a day. This will prevent infestations and diseases.

Use the right fertilizer for your plants. They each have their own tastes. Some prefer potassium, others more phosphorus or nitrogen.

Remove weeds as soon as you see them. Don't let them take advantage of your good soil and choke your lovelies.

Companion planting is like a symbiotic friendship. They help one another by adding habitat for friendly insects, nutrition, maximizing space, pest control, pollination, and productivity. Humans have used this method of farming for thousands of years.

Large plants provide shade for smaller plants. Veggies that spread on the ground, like pumpkins, prevent weed growth. Upright plants go well with these to maximize space. Certain plants go well with each other to provide nutrients for the other. Some plants with long roots bring the nutrients to plants with shallow roots. When planning your 'farm,' consider how long plants take to harvest. Grow plants that grow fast between slower growing plants. You will harvest them first before the slow guys need the room for themselves.

Probably the oldest combination are the three sisters; beans, corn, and squash. The beans add nitrogen. They need the stalk of corn to grow. Corn needs a lot of nitrogen. Squash provides pricky leaves that repel some pests, and shades roots of the other two so they stay cool and keep weeds away. Adding a fourth sister of sunflowers helps save corn for you. Birds see them first because they are taller and eat them instead. They also attract insect pollinators and provide additional support for beans.

Additional information about companion planting to repulse pesky pests and insects from eating your garden is in the Peaceful Pest and Disease Control chapter.

Learn specifics about what you plan on growing. There are some who don't like each other. When growing, cabbage and cauliflower don't get along, just like garlic and beans, even though they are great cooked together.

Pruning is important. By removing dead leaves, more air can circulate, allowing your plants room to grow. They concentrate energy on growing healthy stems, thus giving you higher yields of food. Your lovelies will stay healthy and pests and disease will find it harder to attack. Disinfect your shears to not spread any disease.

# SASSY FOOD
Ja-ne de Abreu

Bees are vital for this planet. Without them we would not have as much food, as well as other plants and flowers. They are the best pollinators and some make honey! They play an integral part in about 70% of the agriculture on the planet. So you can imagine without them, we would have a LOT less food. Pesticides are their biggest enemy. If you use it to save your garden from pests, you are killing friendly insects that help you too. Planting flowers to attract bees is a great way to have nature work for you. Double great whammy is to plant particular herbs and flowers that attract bees while also repelling pesky pests.

Some old houses have beehives built in as an easy way to collect honey. Many different styles of beehives are available ready-made. Simply stick them in your yard, preferably where they get morning sun. Shade or not is dependent on your climate. Providing a home will help bee populations grow and you can have free honey. A bee house in your garden acts as a free hotel. They will love your garden for it. Keep it clean and dry or bees will die during their stay. Purchasing organic products helps save bee populations. Not just food, but anything made from plants like organic cotton, among many other products.

There are over 200,000 species of pollinators like ants, beetles, butterflies, flies, ladybugs, moths, and wasps. Some are friendly for your garden and will aid in eating aphids and other pests. Others (or their larvae) are enemies and will damage your plants and crops. Relocating caterpillars is an example of how to save your garden while saving them also. Keep watch or they will have a party.

When pollinators aren't around (especially in indoor gardens), hand pollination is the next best thing. First you have to identify your flowers. Male flowers are the ones with a little booty and a pollen covered stamin. Female flowers have a big booty and a stigma. Long story short — get the pollen on the stigma. Use a paint brush, cotton tip on a stick, sing to them, turn on the disco lights, whatever it takes. Soon enough you'll see if it worked.

# SASSY FOOD
Ja-ne de Abreu

SASSY FOOD
Ja-ne de Abreu

# Tantalizing Tools

Now that you know what to do, how are you going to do it? Similar to intelligent primates, we use tools to make our work easier. What will you grow and how? Having a special space for your supplies is key to preventing a messy look. While sometimes messy hair is sexy, messy spaces never are.

For sprouts and microgreens, a spray bottle, gardening gloves, plant markers, waterproof gloves, and ceramic scissors are all you'll need.

Hydroponics and aquaponic do not require a large tool list. It's a good idea to have a bucket, gallon container, hydrogen peroxide (food grade), siphon, scissors, spray bottles, and waterproof gloves.

The list is widely variable for container 'farms.' It depends if they are indoors or outside. What size are you planning? Will you use a wall to go vertical? You'll need a trellis for the plants to grow upwards. Small space? Use vertical containers on wheels. Will you utilize a water system or olla balls for easier watering or use a hose or watering can? Is it too hot and sunny? Use a shade sail for success.

If you have small containers, hand tools are great to use. Buckets, forks, gloves, hand shovels, knives, scissors, shears, spades, and trowels are also useful.

*Plant markers are vital to remember their names. It's easy to forget what you planted where.*

# SASSY FOOD
Ja-ne de Abreu

Large containers may require additional larger shears and shovels, along with wheeled plant stands to move them around. A small greenhouse with raised beds can be a good option. I added bamboo trellises to larger containers by drilling a few holes and attaching with zip ties. They are great for vertical growing. Think outside the box for creative solutions. It applies here as well as everywhere in life.

Alcohol and hydrogen peroxide are great to sterilize your tools.

Olla balls have been used over 4,000 years. Bury them with your plants. The porous walls of the clay allow for slow water dispersion.

Tools required for in-ground 'farms' again depends on your size. If it's a small area, use the same tools as containers. Adding tools like an auger, cultivator, hoe, pickax, rake, or tiller, depending on your location and soil, can make growing food easier for you.

If you are going macroscale, a pickup truck and tractor are key. Green houses, high tunnels, and hoop houses are useful in most climates. Might I kindly suggest studying more detailed material about growing large than this book.

SASSY FOOD
Jane de Abreu

# Peaceful Pest & Disease Control

We live in a non-perfect world. Just as we have challenges, the same applies for our beloved plants. For every beautiful plant out there, exists many insects and diseases wanting to feed off of it. The tastier, the more popular. There are ways to combat this, so we can actually eat the plants we are trying so hard to grow, and not just feed these pesky beings.

Grow with your plants. See the small changes. Check them at least twice a day. A lot happens from day to night and also from night to day. For instance, when my okra starts to get about as big as my thumb, I watch it carefully twice a day. They have growth spurts and in a 12-hour period can grow too big to where they are tough and less tasty.

I can also see aphids or mildew spots starting to appear on my plants. It's just a few black specks or white spots at first. If I wash it right away, the plant changes from dull and wilty to gleaming pretty. If I leave it, before I realize, the problem is too big to fix. The plant has to be removed or the problem can quickly spread to other plants and half my garden can be destroyed in a very short time. What to do? It is a tricky balance taking experimentation with each plant and your location.

Cinnamon is a great antifungal. Make a cinnamon tea and spray to prevent rust on larger plants.

Sprinkle powdered cinnamon on soil when planting for a wide variety of benefits, like deterring ants, rabbits, and rodents as well as keeping whiteflies and other pests away.

Some people do not like to kill any living beings. This is where companion planting is useful. We covered other aspects of it in cultivation. Now, let's see how it relates to pest control. Many flowers and herbs repulse insects and other beings who want to eat your food. It is a win-win. You benefit from eating the herbs and have flowers to make your home fresh and your plants stay healthy.

Basil repulses aphids, flies, mosquitoes, and spider mites and controls the tomato hornworm and asparagus beetle. Bees love these flowers.

Chrysanthemum flowers make a wonderful tea and also are an excellent pest control weapon for veggies. They repulse aphids, cabbage worms, leafhoppers, and pickleworms.

Citronella is great to shoo away mosquitoes and other insects.

Coriander benefits all vegetables by repulsing aphids and is delicious.

# SASSY FOOD
Ja-ne de Abreu

Lavender is an all-around amazing plant. It repulses insects and some animals, provides beautiful flowers, and calms you with its scent.

Lemongrass works well in repulsing aphids and mosquitos. It's also useful in the kitchen!

Marigolds repulse a wide range of harmful insects.

Nasturtiums are beautiful and tasty. Plant near veggies and fruit trees. They repulse cucumber beetles, fruit tree borers, squash bugs, and white flies.

Parsley is great to grow near asparagus, carrots, and tomatoes and repulses carrot flies and beetles.

Petunias repulse bean beetles.

Rosemary is good to plant near beans, cabbage, and carrots. It repulses cabbage moths and carrot flies.

Sage is an excellent veggie pest repulse weapon.

Thyme is a good weapon to place near cabbage to control maggots and moths.

Beans add nitrogen to the soil and are yummy. They repulse some enemy insects.

Onions are also useful in the war against pests.

Trap crops are used to plant near your food plants. Insects will be drawn to eat those. When they are overrun, simply remove them. Be careful of the friendly insects that are also attracted if you do throw them away. For example, plant radish near cabbage. Instead of eating your cabbage, insects will eat the radish. Since radish grows quickly, you can plant some of your own elsewhere. Each climate is different. Learn what works best for you.

Crushed eggshells provide calcium and slugs don't like it.

Salt spray is an excellent way to increase absorption of magnesium, phosphorus, and sulfur. Sprinkle salt around the base of the plants. Slugs hate it!

Garlic does more than just repulse vampires. Add some to water and let it sit for a while. Adding onion juice and cayenne aids to help insects flee.

Eucalyptus oil is a more attractive smell for humans, and yet effective in repulsing insects. Spray generously often.

Chrysanthemum flower tea is great for you to drink and also for protecting your garden. Put cooled tea in a spray bottle. Add neem oil for greater effect to protect your plants.

# SASSY FOOD
Ja-ne de Abreu

# SASSY FOOD
## Ja-ne de Abreu

Soap and water go a long way. It's essential to wash our hands in this pandemic. A LOT! This also applies to bathing your plants. Use a natural soap because harsh soap can damage your skin, it can also damage your delicate plants. One or two teaspoons of soap mixed with water in a quart spray bottle and you can wash away aphids, beetles, mites, whiteflies, etc. Add two teaspoons of neem oil to this mix for extra protection. It's great for controlling mildews and many fungi that can decimate your plants. It's a good idea to do this when the challenge first begins for it can quickly get out of control.

Neem oil is a popular option. It's particularly effective in the beginning of an infestation. It inhibits the growth cycle of insects. It is also popular for human skin and hair care. But the smell of the oil may take getting some getting used to (the leaf is also a very powerful medicine for humans in many ways).

There are vast DIY options using citronella, lemongrass, peppermint, and witch hazel. Look up effective recipes to combat the pests that bug your plants.

Vinegar is wonderful for deterring many pests. Use three parts water to one part vinegar as a spray. While this is good for weeds, your plants can get damaged. There are other useful options to spray on your plants instead. Another great thing to do with vinegar is to soak old rags and place it around your in-ground and outdoor raised bed 'farm.' It will deter many animals from munching on your plants..

Some harsher organic weapons are:

Spinosad kills many garden pests. Spray in the evening to reduce killing bees and other friendly insects.

Diatomaceous Earth is best when used dry. It has sharp edges to kill insects. But use caution because it will also kill friendly insects.

Rotenone is slow acting, organic, and moderately toxic to mammals, so use with care.

Just because it's organic doesn't mean it's always good for you. Use protective glasses and waterproof gloves. Please always wear a mask. These days, it's almost weird if we aren't wearing one anyway.

I was excited when I bought the seeds. She was so pretty with multicolored stripes and seemed like she would grow well here. Some people told me it's too rainy on the part of the island where I live. I wanted to try anyway. Only ten seeds arrived. Giving two each to four other sassy food farmers, I planted mine.

Every day I nourished them to seedlings in a newspaper pot, then planted them where they grew big and healthy. When I saw the first tiny delicate yellow flowers, I wanted to call everyone! Diligently I watched for female flowers. It seemed to take forever. When they arrived, I hand pollinated. I almost had a party when I saw the first fruits. People stopping by for quick trades could not leave without seeing her. The taste of the first tiny melon was like an intense honeydew!

A threat of a hurricane caused me to move my container. My lovelies didn't like that. One died and the other thrived. I danced when I saw her first flowers (always male) and danced again when I saw females. I hand pollinated. I saw the start of fruits. Then from one day to the next, she turned dull and drooped. Maybe I forgot to water? No. By nighttime, I knew she wouldn't recover. I almost cried when I had to remove her. Almost eight months of diligent care, and now she's gone. But life always continues. I amended the soil and planted again with beets. As I see their daily growth, I'm happy. I'm still a little sad my melon is gone. And I can try again.

I lost a quick battle of disease with my dear Kajari melon.

# Honorable Harvest

Ja-ne de Abreu

How long do you wait before your food is ready to eat? It depends on what you're growing. Any type of leaves, stems, and roots are best young. That's when they are tender and tasty. Most fruits, however, are best to ripen where they are growing, so the sugar can develop. Think of eating a pineapple in Prague versus a pineapple fresh in Hawai'i? Pineapples don't grow in Prague, so they have to be sent there while green. As a result, they are not nearly as delicious as the pineapples I pick in my yard. That's the difference.

There is something in the way you harvest your food. Treat it with care. Use shears or scissors that are sterilized. If there is any disease, it won't pass along to the next plant your shears touch. Lettuce and other greens love ceramic scissors and won't brown as they do with metal. Or better yet, use your hands.

**SASSY FOOD**
Ja-ne de Abreu

# Playful Propagation

The cycle of growing food continues. Just as all life. After all, it's not one harvest you are after, right? Cuttings, seeds, grafting, division, and layering are ways to make more food.

You can start your 'farm' with cuttings from vegetables bought at the store. That's what I did with potatoes and sweet potatoes (organic only). I also planted seeds from papaya and squash received from trading and had good luck. So, save and dry seeds from your organic produce. Plant them and see if they grow.

Many plants can grow from cuttings. For example, I let a few sweet potatoes hang around and after a while they start to bud. I cut the end off and plant it. Then cook the rest. Romaine lettuce, onions, and celery can be started in water to develop roots before planting. Pretty much any herbs or leafy greens with taproots can grow in this manner. Pineapple or beets are the opposite. Cut the top and stick it in water or directly in soil. Leave a little of the fruit on it and see the magic happen.

Another way to propagate is to cut excess vines and root them. For instance, with sweet potato vines, 6-12 inches are the best. Root them in a vase of water. Once the roots grow over half an inch, they are ready for planting. Many colder climates bring these indoors over the winter to keep in vases and then plant outside after the frost is gone. Most cuttings have root nodes, but some do not and will still root. Change the water every couple of days or you'll have a mess. You can try to root the cutting directly in soil, but my experience is less successful than rooting it in water first. Besides, I like to see the beginning of more life! And more food!

Dip cuttings in cinnamon for a natural root hormone.

# SASSY FOOD
Ja-ne de Abreu

# SASSY FOOD
## Ja-ne de Abreu

Layering is another technique to get your vines to root. Simply bend the vine into the soil and there you go, more roots will grow and so will more food. I do this with my sweet potato plants, and it works well. Herbs also like layering, but need a little help. Scrape the side of the stem with a knife and put it in the soil; that will do the trick. A weight can be useful so it doesn't pop back up.

Division is greater than multiplication? It is in this magical world of planting. Division is used to separate larger plants into smaller ones, so they will grow into full plants of their own. Essentially, you carefully separate the roots and clumps of stems that are growing together. Plant them a distance away or put in separate pots and share or even better, trade. This is best for perennials and bulbs. Taproots like to multiply through cuttings or seeds. Some herbs and other plants growing in clumps can be successfully separated to spread the love on your 'farm.'

Grafting is a way to bring many fruit trees to grow better fruit more quickly (years quicker) and have higher yields (over 30%). They need to be in the same family because like attracts like. The stock is the receiver of the graft and the scion is the graftee, as it were. You attach the scion to the stock and wait patiently. There are differences in grafting methods for the kind of plant and time of year. Learn more details about what you want to add to your 'farm' before you try this for best results.

SASSY FOOD
Ja-ne de Abreu

# Content Cleaning

Just like people, produce love a bath and they pass that love onto you. There are noticeable differences after cleansing when you look at it, touch it, smell it, and taste it. Most people rinse produce in plain water. With increasing sensitivities out there, might I suggest washing with a cleaning agent? There might be an insect that crawled on it and one could have a reaction. If the food is grown indoors, don't have that fear. A quick rinse and they're gleaming. If something is dirty like greens grown outside and root vegetables, rinse the excess dirt off first. Then they are able to have a better bath. Root veggies also need a brush for exfoliation to shine clean. Ones with natural bristles work great.

There are many good store-bought cleansers available. And inexpensive homemade options are so easy, try it to see how DIY can be more convenient and cost effective than hunting down a cleanser in the store. I love natural food and likewise love natural cleansing.

One simple way is with citric acid, which is found to be antimicrobial. This can be in the form of lemon juice. It kills bacteria, germs, and mold. Mix some in a bowl of water and soak your produce for 15 minutes, then rinse.

Vinegar kills bacteria. Proportions are one part vinegar to three parts water.

Baking soda is also excellent at removing any pesticides. Take a small amount and scrub it directly on something with a harder surface like an avocado or potato. For delicate foods such as greens or peaches, dissolve ¼ teaspoon baking soda in a bowl of water and soak 15 minutes, then rinse.

Mix it up! Combine vinegar and lemon for a nicer scent and more thorough cleaning. Put a batch in a spray bottle for those veggies needing a scrub down. Baking soda can also be added.

Produce always love a cold-water bath. Hot water can aid microorganisms entering into them, and therefore, you.

You will feel the difference with your happier produce. The cleaner the produce, the cleaner your body. After all, you are what you eat!

# Compassionate Composting

*Make tea with banana peels. Then compost the peels.*

Composting is perceived as dirty, smelly, and messy. This is a big misnomer. Yes, if you have an open pile outside with a covering of leaves, things can become rank. That is why they are placed in a far corner of a yard. Nowadays, there are tiny units that don't smell with no mess that anyone can compost even in an apartment without a balcony.

Why do this? Because it is a good way to return the inedible parts of produce, scraps, leaves, cardboard, etc, etc, etc, back to become earth. And that grows more food for you. It is a natural cycle.

Since the pandemic began, I started composting. It diminished the amount of trash. I use the soil for my containers. My system catches the 'tea' and I pour a little in all my container plants and they love it! What can be composted? Vegetable and fruit scraps like peels, seeds, and stems, whole grains, eggshells, old food except meat and dairy, tea leaves, coffee grinds, toilet paper rolls, and other non-bleached thin cardboard, leaves, grass clippings, and small sticks. The ratio for optimal compost is generally 1/3 food to 2/3 paper and leaves. Too much in either direction leads to a nasty mess. One way to tell is by the smell — freshhh, which is a great motto.

Some cities and companies are now providing services to pick up your compost. They offer a range of services; dropping it off yourself or pickups at residences, a group pickup in a residential area, office or high rise pick up, or restaurant pick up. Imagine if this was implemented in all cities? How much waste would be reduced!?!

# SASSY FOOD
Jane de Abreu

Many community gardens appreciate compost, even if you aren't a member. It's a great way to help others and the environment without much effort.

Restaurants can provide compost to farms. Maybe you can drop off yours individually to a local farmer or barter a trade, which is increasingly popular in the pandemic. Maybe trading will stick as one of the positive permanent changes out of these crazy times?

When there was an international shortage of paper towels and toilet paper, I immediately switched to cloth napkins and microfiber cleaning rags. I had wanted to do this for a long time, but thought it was costly and complicated. Since the pandemic began caregiving, cleaning, and cooking takes up most of my time. For safety reasons, no one is allowed inside. Since I have little time to go out it is easier to buy food in bulk. Almost everything we eat is made from scratch now. We are healthier as a result.

Our trash consumption is reduced from several bags of trash a week to one. It is incredible how much of a difference is made with a few simple changes! It is a tiny investment to start, but it saves more money over time. Most of us say 'yes we have climate change and we need to do something about it.' And our lives are so busy we then think, 'we will do it tomorrow' or 'it's a nice thought but I won't make that much of a difference' and order take-out. If we each take responsibility for ourselves and do our individual part, we can change the world. With wildfires raging out of control and increasing hurricanes, along with other increasing horrific natural disasters, things are spiraling out of control. We can change that, and we all need to participate. Small changes add up quickly.

A small can with a filtered lid in the kitchen makes things easier. Deposit it in your compost system once a day for best results.

Let's meander the maze of composters: One popular option is barrels that spin. There are many sizes and styles from which to choose. Adding an activator will speed the breakdown by adding nitrogen, phosphorus, and potassium. Most of these can be placed close to the house; some units are smell-proof indoor varieties. These range from $35-$200. While most come in black to maximize the heat from the sun, I couldn't resist one in pretty pink.

Vermicomposting is having worms as your friends to help break down organic waste. They help aerate and keep water in the soil. They grow well in many of these systems as well as growing in your larger containers and raised beds. The soil they leave behind is very rich and your plants love this kind of luxury.

Kobayashi is different from all others with its fermentation system. It uses special equipment and in ten days has usable material. Meat and dairy scraps can be utilized here. Layering wheat germ, wheat bran, or sawdust with molasses along with your food in this airtight system can be done in a bucket in a tiny space. Once set up, maintenance is easy. And being anaerobic, there's no smell. A spigot at the bottom of the bucket makes it easy to use the 'tea' for your farm. This can be built DIY or complete kits are available.

SASSY FOOD
Ja-ne de Abreu

There are systems which you place in the ground (most utilize the benefit of worms). The underground method leaches nutrients directly to your garden, eliminating the need to take it out and spread it around yourself.

Keyhole gardens are a great way to grow food and be able to compost together as discussed earlier in the Carefree Containers chapter.

Other DIY methods:
Simple inexpensive wire bin made in 10 minutes. Fill with leaves and start composting.

Trash bin or plastic bin with lids. Fill with leaves and place food scraps.

A barrel fitted with bicycle wheels on each end works well. Cut and hinge a door and there ya go!

If you are growing ground beds, consider sheet composting. By layering your compost near the beds, the nutrients are immediately received.

If using one of the more traditional methods of composting, 90% dry material like leaves and unbleached thin cardboard like toilet paper rolls to 10% wet material is best.

If disposing of a plant that is diseased or has pests on it, use other means for disposal, like the recycle waste bin or trash bin. If not, the disease could get back into your soil and cause problems for your future plants.

**SASSY FOOD**
Ja-ne de Abreu

# Flowy Foraging

Foraging is not technically growing food, but it is a wonderful way to enhance being in nature. The food you find is completely organic, of course, and free. It is delicious and fun to collect and share!

First of all, please know the food you are picking. If you aren't sure, leave it alone, for it could be poisonous. I have a reputation of being a good fruit hunter in Hawai'i. I know which trails have what fruit. When on a trail, I track my 'prey' by spotting color amongst the green or a fallen fruit, then following the signs to the tree or vine and voila! Climbing trees and crouching low are some of the key ways to stay agile and spot 'prey'. When harvesting, please be mindful of the creatures in the wild that need the 'prey' as a food source. You are a visitor in their home, so please leave some for them.

Collecting fruit in the wild is a great way to assist with the invasive plant problem. Think of it as the vegetarian method of population control.

Bring a knife and bags to help harvest..

# SASSY FOOD
### Ja-ne de Abreu

Some people plant in the wild. While it is not something I promote, it is a pretty cool idea. What is amazing is growing fruit trees as shade trees in public areas. Some communities have started doing this. It helps everyone have more access to free food, especially people who need it most.

Foraging is a wonderful thing to do in every part of the world. We each have our own special foods. Before 'civilization' we were hunters and gatherers. Where did we gather? Exactly. In Hawaii, we are fortunate to have avocado, banana, breadfruit, coconuts, coffee, guava, kukui nuts, lilikoi, limu, macadamia nuts, mango, and mountain apples. What do you have where you live? So return to your roots. For the time we are in the wild, whether we realize it or not, we flow with nature and our ancestors.

Ja-ne de Abreu

# Food is Music

Page 148

# SASSY FOOD
## Ja-ne de Abreu

You planted seeds, cultivated your plants, protected them from disease and pests, watched them lovingly, and harvested them. Now the time is here! To eat what you grew! But how? As the pace of people in 'civilized' communities sped up, the connection with growing food and preparing it slowed down. Restaurants, take away, and processed foods became more popular to the point of many not knowing how to cook anything fresh. Let's get things grooving in the other direction. It can be easy. With the pandemic, many people are forced to stay home and do things they never thought possible, including cooking.

My body is a delicate, petite frame like a classical melody and my spirit is a fierce funky force. The kitchen is one area where people see my true soul. When I started learning about preparing food, creating my own melodies with spices and herbs was vital for me. It's like a moving meditation. After much practice, I can now make a light arabesque, or an intense opera, or a complex samba, or a unique rhythm all its own. Let's explore how to create a beat with flexible cooking.

Here are some instruments:

- Almond
- Allspice
- Anise
- Apple
- Basil
- Bay Leaves
- Blueberry
- Capers
- Carambola (Star fruit)
- Cardamom
- Carraway
- Cayenne
- Chili Powder
- Cilantro
- Cinnamon
- Cloves
- Coconut
- Coriander
- Cranberry
- Cumin
- Curry
- Dates
- Dill
- Fennel
- Fenugreek
- Filé Gumbo
- Garlic
- Ginger
- Kaffir lime
- Honey
- Lavender
- Lemon
- Lime
- Mace
- Maple Syrup
- Marjoram
- Mint
- Molasses
- Mustard
- Nutmeg
- Olives
- Onion
- Orange
- Oregano
- Paprika
- Parsley
- Persimmon
- Peppercorns
- Pomegranate
- Poppy Seed
- Rose
- Rosemary
- Saffron
- Salt
- Sage
- Sesame
- Star Anise
- Sugar
- Sumac
- Tahini
- Tangerine
- Tamarind
- Tarragon
- Thyme
- Turmeric
- Vanilla
- Vinegar
- Zaatar

# SASSY FOOD
Ja-ne de Abreu

This is a broad list. Just like many instruments there are many variations. How many different kinds of drums exist? So here, lemon can be fresh, frozen, juice, powder, or pulp. Almond can be whole or sliced, turned into milk, or butter. You get the theme. Curry powder and garam masala are a blend of spices and commonly available. Use them or make your own. And by the way, curry leaves are unique and not related to curry powder. Try them both to see.

With this partial list, we can cook like we are in Brazil, Greece, Jamaica, India, Italy, Morocco, and many other countries. Depending on my mood, I use more or less ingredients and amounts. When cooking, listening to music from the country of the food enhances the experience.

Yes, it can be confusing. At first. Like listening to unfamiliar rhythms from an unknown country with indecipherable lyrics. As you turn off your mind and feel with your soul, you'll enter into that rhythm and know the vibration of the words. And in this case, the food.

## SASSY FOOD
### Ja-ne de Abreu

Use your senses. Smell the spices. As you are cooking, imagine what else would go well with it. Think of the country you are visiting in your mind. Imagine the feel you want to experience. Taste it, close your eyes, and pause. The ingredient will come to you. Add little amounts at a time. Smell how it changes your song. Taste it again. Wait to experience the notes on the back of your throat. Pause again. How do you feel inside? See how the colors change too. When it's well rounded, your masterpiece is finished. I create every day in this way. Experiment with me.

Vegetables can be simple, and most take a short time to prepare. Here are some to get started:
green beans, long beans, beets, broccoli, brussels sprouts, cabbage, carrots, cauliflower, chard, collard greens, eggplant, kale, mirliton (aka chayote), mustard greens, peas, potatoes, spinach, squash, sweet potatoes, turnips, turnip greens, and zucchini can be baked, boiled, broiled, roasted, steamed, or stir fried.

You can use one of these instruments or several: basil, cardamom, cilantro, cinnamon, cloves, coriander, cumin, dill, fennel, garlic, ginger, lemon, lime, marjoram, nutmeg, orange, oregano, parsley, pepper, rosemary, salt, sage, sesame seeds, sumac, tarragon, thyme, zaatar.

If you're going to use all of them, you'll need a LOT of veggies or a tiny sprinkle of instruments. Mix it up. Experiment. You'll find your tune.

Here are some basic recipes. You can use the recipe as is or morph it with Exotica options or create your own. Use all or some of the ingredients listed in one of the boxes. Let your senses be the guide to show what amounts are right for you.

**SASSY FOOD**
Ja-ne de Abreu

# Shakarkandi

Let's start with a simple Indian raga — Shakarkandi

Sweet Potatoes
Lime juice
Cumin
Salt

Wash and brush the sweet potatoes. Poke holes in the skin with a fork. Roast in the oven in a pan with water covering the bottom. Cook at 425° F for 60-90 minutes until caramel starts to ooze out of the holes. Let cool.

Unwrap and mash with or without the skin, adding equal amounts of lime juice and cumin, and a dash of salt. Be bold and you'll be rewarded!

SASSY FOOD
Ja-ne de Abreu

# Smashed Potatoes

Now moving on to a sultry Bossa Nova — dairy free Smashed Potatoes (Exotica options):

Potatoes
Salt
Coconut milk and/or almond milk
Non-dairy buttery spread

Wash and brush the potatoes. Cut into large uniform chunks. Place in a pot of water. Boil until soft. Test with a fork. Drain. Return potatoes to the pot.

Add equal amounts of coconut and almond milk or use just one kind. Add a large dollop of a non-dairy buttery spread and sprinkle salt. Mash. I use an immersion blender for ultimate smoooooth.

Exotica options - use some or all ingredients in one of the boxes:

garlic
pepper

basil
oregano
tarragon

Sauté in olive oil combo of any below or all:

| | | |
|---|---|---|
| cardamom | curry powder | diced carrots |
| cinnamon | ginger | diced onions |
| cloves | nutmeg | peas |
| coriander | pepper | lemon juice |
| cumin | turmeric | |

Mix with potatoes

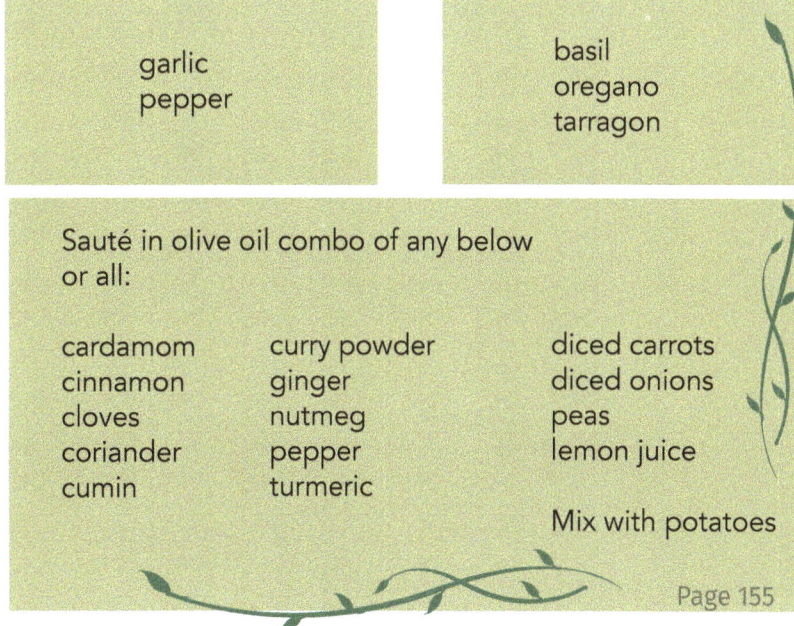

# Oba! Okra

Many people have issues with okra because it's slimy. And it doesn't have to be, depending on how you cook it. Okra is special for me. I ate it in New Orleans where I was raised. Enjoyed it in Brazil, the land of my parents. Loved it when visiting Jamaica. And gulped it down in India, where I have hanai family. Okra is nutritious and some studies suggest it's a possible antidiabetic agent. There are a thousand ways to cook this magic wonder. One simple ditty is to use a skillet, best if it's cast iron.

Add a little regular olive oil (not virgin or extra virgin). Wash and cut your okra into slices. Put the heat on medium high until it's hot.

Add:
okra
salt

Stir fry until it starts to turn brown and you're done. You'll see the slime oozing. Just cook it a little more until it's gone.

# SASSY FOOD
## Jane de Abreu

Experiment with just one of these Exotica options. Then try it again with a couple. You'll see how different they taste. And it's always scrumptious!

basil
cinnamon
cumin
curry powder
ginger

A different saucy melody is to start as before. If using just cast iron, don't add tomatoes or lemon juice (substitute with vegetable broth) or use a regular skillet instead. If using cast iron with an enamel coating, you're all good.

Instrument list:
olive oil
okra
onions and/or garlic
allspice
cardamom
cinnamon
cloves
cumin
ginger (powder or diced)
nutmeg
pepper
salt
tomatoes
lemon juice
vegetable broth
bay leaves

Sauté onions and/or garlic. Add allspice, ginger, cinnamon, nutmeg, cardamon, cloves, and pepper. After it caramelizes, add okra. After a few minutes add one or more vegetable broth, lemon juice, and tomatoes until it's very saucy. Break one or two bay leaves and turn down the heat to simmer until it's thickened. Depending on the amount of okra and sauce, up to thirty minutes. Serve over grits, polenta, quinoa, or rice.

# SASSY FOOD
Ja-ne de Abreu

Page 158

# Liquid Sunshine

SASSY FOOD
Ja-ne de Abreu

Let's move on to fruit. Some fruits are high in pectin which is what makes jam thick and some are low. If you use only low pectin fruits it won't thicken well and won't be a thick jam, but you can call it compote and it's perfect. Adding sugar will thicken things, along with reducing the sauce. It can also get thick if you add lemon juice. Mixing low and high pectin fruits is a great option.

Powdered pectin is another way to thicken your creation. Add it to your cold juice or fruit before heating. Heat it to a rolling boil and then add sugar.

Higher Pectin Fruits:
apples, blueberries, boysenberries, carrots, citrus, cranberries, currants, gooseberries (poha), papaya, plums (not Italian), raspberries, sour cherries

Lower Pectin Fruits:
apricots, blackberries, carambola, figs, grapes, guavas, italian plums, peaches, pears, pineapple, pomegranates, rhubarb, strawberries

If you want your fruits soft, boil your fruit with some lemon juice before adding hot sugar. Place sugar in a pan in the oven until it's hot to touch (10-15 min). Watch it or it will melt and caramelize.

If you want your fruits candied, add room temperature sugar to the pan with the fruits then put the pan on the stove.

This jazzy number is great to ward off the funk of cold weather blues. Place a teaspoon (or more) in a cup of hot water as a tea. Serve it over ice cream. Spread it on toast. Mix it with soda water or rum. Or… you tell me.

Liquid Sunshine (Exotica options)
Citrus options (and/or):
calamansi
kumquat
lime
lemon
orange
peeled diced ginger
tangerine

Plus
sugar
lemon juice if needs more zest.

Peel citrus and slice fruit into small cubes. The white part of rinds will increase bitterness, and is your choice to keep or discard. Place in a pot. Add ginger (can get hot if you use a lot). Pour a generous amount of sugar. Bring to a boil. Lower heat to low to medium low until juice is reduced. When it's at 220° F it is supposed to be set. But mine is set at a lower temperature. If you don't have a candy thermometer, place a small plate in the freezer when you begin. To test it, take the plate out, and drop a little jam on it. Wait half a minute. If it wrinkles when you move it, it's ready.

cardamom, cinnamon, cloves, honey molasses, nutmeg

**SASSY FOOD**
Ja-ne de Abreu

# Star Blues

Another Bluesy Jam is Star Blues (Exotica options). I use dried apricots and frozen blueberries because it is what's available in Hawai'i. If you don't have access to star fruit, skip it or add apples, cranraisins, kiwi, or pears. If you don't have blueberries, use strawberries or cherries. No apricots? Skip it or use another fruit. Getting the hang of flexible cooking? Try the cranberry option to jazz up your holiday gathering (until the pandemic is over, maybe give take away jars?). Add nuts, like roasted pecans or macadamia nuts, for an extra zest.

carambola (star fruit)
apricots
blueberries
sugar

Wash and slice star fruit into stars. Add diced apricots and blueberries. Pour in a generous amount of sugar. Bring to a boil. Lower heat to low to medium low until liquid is half reduced. How many blueberries you use will depend on the liquid you need to reduce because it contains the pectin needed to thicken. In a short while, you have something extraordinary. After it cools, if it's too thick, don't fret. Add a little warm water to lighten it up. If it's too thin, don't fret either. Boil it more to jam or call it compote. When the liquid reaches 220° F it is supposed to be set, but mine is set at lower temperatures. If you don't have a candy thermometer, place a small plate in the freezer when you get started. To test, take the plate out, and drop a little jam on it. Wait half a minute. If it wrinkles when you move it, it's ready.

allspice, cardamom, cinnamon, cloves, ginger, nutmeg

**SASSY FOOD**
Ja-ne de Abreu

# Screaming Ice Cream

Now for the big finale.

Screaming Ice Cream (Exotica options)
This is a significant flexible force. Like most music, let's start with the bass.

1 qt coconut milk (I make my own from powder and make it extra creamy) or
1qt almond milk (I make my own from a paste)

1 can coconut cream (the one I use is an organic box kind or I make my own)

½ -1 can coconut condensed milk (or I make my own)

1-2 tsp. vanilla (I almost always add and occasionally omit depending on options)

Mix in a blender.

From there, options seem endless:

Add any fruit or combinations therein. Avocado is a great choice.

Add any fruit syrup or jam.

Heat up chocolate and/or sliced almonds and mix that in. Add cherries, strawberries, or blueberries to that mix. Or leave the chocolate out.

Add instant coffee.

Add earl grey tea or another favorite.

Add saffron.

Add tahini.

Add rose water and nutmeg.

Add turmeric and cinnamon.

Add chopped cookies.

Add ginger crumble (recipe on my website).

Once you have your concerto, chill it. Then add it to your ice cream machine. Mine is a frozen canister type attachment for my mixer. Thirty minutes later and you're shakin' your booty to the brass band.

More gastronomic stories are on my website, ja-ne.com. They are all gluten and dairy free. I'm continuing to add as time allows. Share your creations with me and I'll put them up, so we can all enjoy our groovy disco tunes.

allspice, cardamon, cinnamon, cloves, ginger, nutmeg

I hope this book is able to help you grow fresh food. It is not a complete all-knowing encyclopedia, but it will get you started. Growing food truly helps me and now is a permanent positive lifestyle. When the pandemic began, I felt the global tension inside my body. My chest hurt and I was always uneasy. Choosing to grow food kept me focused on many positives; learning (a lot in a short time), success (food), and sharing (knowledge and food). My hanai mother loves it. She brags to all her friends that we are sassy girls with a sassy farm. She looks forward to seeing the daily changes. Since she's in the older age category, we rarely leave the house for safety. She used to want to go out and now she's happy to stay in. I show her the harvest and the effects of the depressing news melts away. The world seems to get crazier and we continue to get calmer. Sharing and eating not just fresh food, the fresh food we grew, is significant for us. My wish is it will be for you too. Friends who never imagined growing anything their entire lives are now content with their 'farms'. Like me. We are all together as one human race on this planet and are linked far more than we will ever realize.

As you progress in your growing journey, keep in mind everything you do has an intention. If you simply go through the motions, you'll get food. And it won't be as plentiful and vibrant as when you are mindful of the task you are doing with your plants. Thank the seed and all the people involved that brought the seed to your hands. Thank the plant as it grows for nurturing you. And thank the food when you eat it. Try both ways as an experiment and see for yourself.

You will find during your growing adventure that if diligent, you can add sassy food to your meals every day. I have found in my space it's not enough to only eat from my 'farm'. Trading has become a fun way to expand what I eat. Buying from local farmers is an excellent way to support your community and eat super fresh. Staying local also helps the planet with less CO2 emissions because you are not buying food that has to travel. Our planet is our only home. Where will we go if we destroy it?

Aloha and stay in touch,
Ja-ne

# SASSY FOOD
## Ja-ne de Abreu

This book arrived from a spark of inspiration. It took great collaboration to be able to complete it amidst a global pandemic and election tension. Maintaining social distancing and proper protocols was important throughout. It was like we built a pyramid of positive energy that became larger and stronger with each person who entered our vibration. Almost all elements of the book were made during the dark tense months of October and November 2020. Only creative, fun, happy, sassy, whimsical energy was poured into the designs, photographs, and words. May we all stay in that energy despite all the craziness and stress until this pandemic ends — and beyond. Growing food really does make a difference in many ways.

Layout and graphic design:
Cipriano Mauricio — www.DigitalPondDesign.com

Photographers:
Ja-ne de Abreu — All photos except:

Becca Roach — Food for Thought Eve photo
Candice Box — Aquaponics Eve photo
Yumi Hi — WowWaterWow Eve photo
Cipriano Mauricio — WowWaterWow leaf photo
Twain Newhart — front and back cover photos

Edited by — Moana Tregaskis and Sue Toth

Vegetable graphics courtesy of Vecteezy.com

Eve models in order of appearance:

Kate McClain
Ja-ne de Abreu
Kamele o pu'uwai Donaldson
Natalie Gocobachi
Carin Prechtl
Kyra Grafton
Rose Wolfe
Bruna Smith
Elina Fishman Savage (help with photoshoots)
Elena Kim
Becca Roach
Keema Cooper
Jong Il Lee
Genie Kuniyoshi
Rachel Glassman
Moana McGlaughlin Tregaskis (hanai mother)

Advice and location for photos — Robert Dunn, Scott Fitzel, Mark Hamamoto

From inspiration to creation this book took seven weeks. Are you curious to read what took me seven years to write? My debut novel exploring the mystery of your free will called *The Energy Inside Valsin's Choices* is launching 2021.

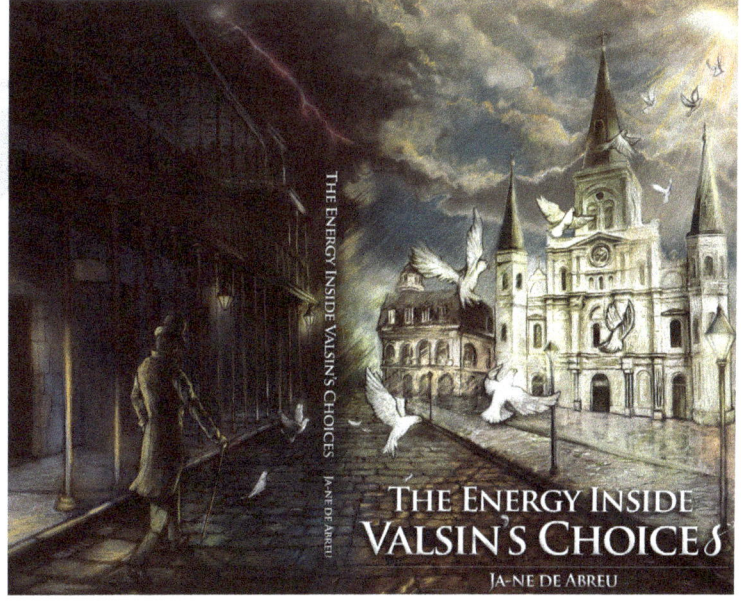

# SASSY FOOD
## Ja-ne de Abreu

### About the Author

Twenty years working with photography, videography, and writing for other companies to fulfill their creative projects prompted Telly award winner, Ja-ne de Abreu, to manifest her own. Ja-ne focuses on exploring the energy inside our choices and the resulting responsibilities and freedoms by telling stories through various mediums. In her spare time she enjoys hanging in jungles of Hawai'i.

Instagram @jmfdea and @sassyfoodfarms

Join the collective at sassyfoodfarms.com
Explore stories at www.ja-ne.com

### JMFdeA Press Books
Building the Bases: Seabees in Southeast Asia
Chasing the Surge
China Bomb: A Novel
The Energy Inside Valsin's Choices
Invasion Diary
Last Plane to Shanghai
Persiguiendo la Oleada
Sassy Food
Seven Leagues to Paradise
Stronger Than Fear
Vietnam Diary
The Warrior King: Hawaii's Kamehameha the Great
Woman and the Sea: Book of Poems
X-15 Diary

www.ingramcontent.com/pod-product-compliance
Lightning Source LLC
Chambersburg PA
CBHW051119110526
44589CB00026B/2980